MAMA AMAZONICA

Pascale Petit was born in Paris, grew up in France and Wales and lives in Cornwall. She is of French/Welsh/Indian heritage. Her eighth collection, *Tiger Girl* (2020), won an RSL Literature Matters Award while in progress, and a poem from the book won the 2020 Keats-Shelley Poetry Prize. *Tiger Girl* was shortlisted for the 2020 Forward Prize for Best Collection and for the English language poetry category shortlist for Wales Book of the Year 2021. Her seventh collection *Mama Amazonica* (Bloodaxe Books, 2017), a Poetry Book Society Choice, won the RSL Ondaatje Prize 2018 and the Laurel Prize 2020. She has published six previous poetry collections, four of which were shortlisted for the T.S. Eliot Prize, most recently, her sixth collection, *Fauverie* (Seren, 2014). A portfolio of poems from that book won the 2013 Manchester Poetry Prize. In 2018 she was appointed as Fellow of the Royal Society of Literature. She received a Cholmondeley Award from the Society of Authors in 2015.

Her fifth collection, *What the Water Gave Me: Poems after Frida Kahlo*, published by Seren in 2010 (UK) and Black Lawrence Press in 2011 (US), was shortlisted for both the T.S. Eliot Prize and Wales Book of the Year. Two of her previous books, *The Zoo Father* and *The Huntress*, were also shortlisted for the T.S. Eliot Prize. In 2004 the Poetry Book Society selected Petit as one of the Next Generation Poets. *The Zoo Father* was a Poetry Book Society Recommendation. A poem from the book, 'The Strait-Jackets', was shortlisted for a Forward Prize.

PASCALE PETIT

Mama Amazonica

BLOODAXE BOOKS

ISBN: 978 1 78037 294 5

First published 2017 by
Bloodaxe Books Ltd,
Eastburn,
South Park,
Hexham,
Northumberland NE46 1BS.

www.bloodaxebooks.com
For further information about Bloodaxe titles
please visit our website or write to
the above address for a catalogue.

Supported using public funding by
**ARTS COUNCIL
ENGLAND**

Digital reprint of the 2017 Bloodaxe Books edition.

For my mother

CONTENTS

Mama Amazonica

1

Picture my mother as a baby, afloat
on a waterlily leaf,

a nametag round her wrist –
Victoria amazonica.

There are rapids ahead
the doctors call 'mania'.

For now, all is quiet –
she's on a deep sleep cure,

a sloth clings to the cecropia tree,
a jaguar sniffs the bank.

My mother on her green raft,
its web of ribs, its underside of spines.

I'll sing her a lullaby,
tell her how her quilted crib

has been known to support
a carefully balanced adult.

My newborn mama
washed clean by the drugs,

a caiman basking beside her.

2

All around her the other patients snore
while her eyes open their mandorlas.

Now my mother is turning
into the flower,

she's heating up. By nightfall
her bud opens its petals

to release
the heady scent of pineapple.

How the jungle storeys stir
in the breeze from the window behind her.

She hears the first roar
of the howler monkey,

then the harpy eagle's swoop,
the crash through galleries of leaves,

the sudden snatch
then the silence in the troop.

   3

Haloperidol,
phenobarbital –

they've tried them all
those witch doctors, and still

she leaps up in her green nightie
and fumbles to make tea,

slopping the cup over her bed
like the queen of rain.

See her change from nightclub singer
to giant bloom

in the glow of the nightlight –

a mezzo-soprano
under the red moon.

She's drawing the night-flying scarabs
into the crucible of her mind.

Over and over they land
and burrow into her lace.

By dawn she closes her petals.

  4
All the next day the beetles stay inside her,
the males mount the females,

their claws hooked round forewings.

There is pollen to feed on –
no need to leave their *pension*.

Night after night, my mother
replays this – how the white

lily of her youth
let that scarab of a man

scuttle into her floral chamber
before she could cry no.

She flushes a deep carmine,
too dirty to get up.

And her face releases them –
the petals of her cheeks spring open.

Black beetles crawl out, up the ward walls.

Jaguar Girl

Her gaze is tipped with curare,

her face farouche
from the kids' asylum

where ice baths
failed to tame her.

Her claws are crescent moons
sharpened on lightning.

She swims through the star-splinters
of a mirror

and emerges snarling –
my were-mama.

She's a rainforest
in a straitjacket.

Where she leaps
the sky comes alive, unleashed
from its bottle.

My mother, trying to conceal
her lithium tremor

as she carries the Amazon
on her back,

her rosettes of rivers
and oxbow lakes,

her clouds of chattering caciques,
her flocks of archangels.

Her own tongue is a hive
that stings

yet pollinates
all the orchids of the forest.

Her ears prick
to the growl of roots

under concrete,
the purr of plants growing.

My Animal Mother,
shaman's bitch,

a highway bulldozed
through her brain,

shapeshifter
into a trembling rabbit
whenever I'm scared of her.

She who has had electric eels
pressed to her scalp

can vanish into backwoods
where no one can reach her.

I'm trying to sew her
back together,

to make a patchwork
of gold dust
and ghost vines,

a sylvan pelt
of torn-down trees,

the shadow dance
of leaves on litter.

I'm trying to conjure her
in her zoo cage

as the doctor comes
running to dart her.

Rainforest in the Sleep Room

1

The highway goes through
the Amazon's brain
like an ice pick through an eye-socket.

First we clear her synapses
then she forgets her animals.

2

Our bulldozers drive through
the rainbow boa of her cortex
like a scalpel –

those sleeping coils
still dreaming up new species,

3

hallucinations we've blitzed
with ECT.

The bilateral current purrs
through her frontal lobes

like a forest of songbirds
electrocuted by rain.

4

Afterwards, her thoughts are nestless,
except for a few chicks
up in the last ironwoods,
patrolled by armed guards.

Scientists climb ropes
to monitor her stats,
bring motherless macaws

down to incubators,
measuring their wings,
weighing naked souls,

5

as if she's a patient
in the Sleep Room
who won't wake –

her dreams treelines
traced by the EEG pen.

6

The only animals left
are grainy films
on camera traps

7

and a recording of the last
musician-wren

whose still small voice
is like the beginning of the world.

Macaw Mummy

Soon they will unwrap her.
Soon it will be over –

only five hundred
years to go.

What did he put in her drink?
Whatever it was has given her

a dream she can't escape from,
however much she wills

the bandages to unwind,
her eyes to open,

however much she promises
never to cry again.

Her scarlet feathers
lie bravely under the ice

of his deep-frozen duvet.

Taxidermy

His sheets smell of formalin.
She feels as if her insides

are outside her, in a freezer.
Instead of a heart

she now has cotton wool,
and where he's stitched her

back together the seams itch.
While she was out cold he scraped

out her eye-sockets to insert
glass eyes she cannot close.

Love Charm

The man who surprises her with a marriage permit
is also the boy who smeared slug slime
on the stems of foxgloves to capture hummingbirds.

The boy who threaded string through one eye
and out the other,
so his little gems would swing round him
and be his playmates,

is also this perfectly coiffed gentleman
who offers her a hummingbird necklace
he's kept since childhood, preserved for this moment.

My Mother's Wedding Dress

I found the remnants of the dress you made
for your wedding to my father –
couldn't imagine the nights spent
in the woods, gathering cobwebs
from bushes, a harvest of
lace spirals, zigzagged orbs
and the hawthorn you picked, choosing
only stems with the longest spines.
I tried to picture you in the mairie
with your groom in his ivory suit.
Years later, you'd say *I married in black*
but I thought of the love needed
to fasten those webs over the thorns.
The steel strength of the spider
must have been your strength
shielding the embryo inside, how once
dew must have glittered on the dirty fabric.
It was as if you'd created night's garments
and were honouring the dark even
as it spun itself around your body
in radials and interstices, a shroud
he would have to tear from you
but only after you had vanished
and the cells that were me
in their crib of silk were abseiled away
under a folded leaf until it was safe.
He would have found your flesh dry
as dust, breasts light as dandelion clocks.
He would have had to crush your necklace
of owl's eggs, your bracelet of moths.

Chaplet

My bridal wreath
is a palisade
circling my face.

I hide in my twig
and thorn wood.
It is my chapel

where I pray to
the king of the forest
to light the flames.

Come, rescuer.
Come as a stag,
with hooves kicking sparks,

antlers like torches.
I must be married
in fire.

By the time the groom
claims his kiss
my hair will fan around us

like the halo
saints wear when
burnt at the stake.

Something Blue

Her dress is pulled over her face
                her veil splayed against starflower bruises

softened now to forget-me-not
                through the lace

a morpho pinned to each temple

the wings drunk
                weighed down
as if by quicksilver

the broken mirror-wings on the long butterfly net
                of her train

he says the bed is a pull-up
                and is set like a spring-trap

should she struggle
                she'll be slammed into the wall

Bestiarum

He comes like ninety
        wolves leaping through air

he is Bête du Gévaudan
        killer-wolf and loup-garou

he comes as a mastiff-hyena cross
        as he flies he catches dogs

mid-air and toys with them
        she is his shepherdess

she'll go on all fours for him
        he'll bite her by the scruff

the bed his watering hole
        for all the night-beasts

you are *mine* he repeats
        you are thinking of *me*

Bandaged Bambi

1 *Bandaged*

In the kitchen with the one gas ring
she has to learn to cook on,
a fawn is helping,
its body tightly bandaged.

2 *Bambi*

Her right leg is in a splint,
as is her left elbow
and he's bandaged up her chest.

She wonders where he's put her breasts
now that she's a fawn.

Only her rump, with its spots like hail,
is exposed to the air.

She remembers the hailstorm,
a mirror shattering
and slivers of ice

snaking towards her.

Love Charm II

He has ground hummingbird bones
into her powder compact,

so that when she gets up
from her dressing-table

her face flies towards him.
The wings of her eyebrows

have that startled expression,
as if flying backwards.

Her cupid's bow quivers
against his kiss

like he's a bird-eating flower.
Picture her, for the rest of her life –

an albino hummingbird,
feathers falling in a snowstorm,

her hair shocked white.

He Gives Her a Nightdress Sheer as a Mist-Net

He insists she changes into it
as soon as they get to the chateau.

She can hear the birds rustling,
wonders how they survived

the gift box, these goldcrests,
linnets. He admires their colours

that match her skin-tones.
Only now does she see that he's

opened all his cages, that birds
are flying around the room,

crashing into the windows
before tangling in her nightie.

He waits until they are exhausted.
Hours pass as he sips brandy.

Only then does the nightingale begin
its nuptial song, piercing

the room with a river of notes
as if it's broken through

into a grove hidden in her breast,
an arbour where it will be safe.

All night it sings and she listens,
all night the forest inside her grows.

Giant Jewel Beetle Ear-Pendants

He hooks forty jewelled wing-cases
from each of her ears,
leads her to the mirror
where she sees herself flanked
by burnished cascades of
giant beetle elytra
tipped with orange toucan feathers.
The glass mists like steam
from an Ecuadorian jungle
as he explains how the larvae
bored through the Shuar's sacred tree
to feed on its fallen wood,
how the shaman hung their captives' heads
from the spirit-house beams
and threaded the insects
to decorate their trophies.
She stares at the bronze cave
of the wardrobe mirror
where he's sewing her lips together,
calls her his Amazonian queen,
says she must be brave, that he'll
stitch her eyes when he's finished.
Her face is becoming wrinkled
as a shrunken doll.
The jewel beetles click their
green and purple forewings
as if chattering to one another –
they have so much to say
about childhoods tunnelling
through dead wood,
so much stored in hindbrains.
Their claws patter on the glass as they mate
but whatever her husband is doing
she no longer feels, now that her body
is numb from the neck down
as if it's been cut off.

Miscarriage

He gives her gin then saffron.
In the toilet she gives birth to a boy.
Afterwards she needs a glass dome
to lie inside, a red balloon tied to her thigh.
The doctor calls it the afterbirth
but she knows it's a balloon
because she can hear it squeak
and besides, her husband bursts it,
then packs her off to work.

Serpentarium

She can fit a thirty-foot giant
into one sheet of A4,

pack pythons
into her sketchbook,

squeezing their loops
in tight breeding-balls, until

the man comes with his forked stick
and pins her head down.

She must have been drawing
too fast, her tail in her mouth

like Ouroboros – that's
what they call her when

she goes crazy. Years ago
they sewed up

her mouth. Now,
a nurse comes to unstitch her.

He nails her head on a hook,
but that's just the beginning, she

knows it gets worse.
She thinks if she can draw

enough snakes she'll get
used to it, stop her eyes blinking

when he shoves the hose
down her throat, makes the room tilt,

water poured into her stomach,
her jaws unhinged. Three of them

holding her down
to strap her arms to her chest,

while she thrashes against the memory –
always the same memory

of the reptile she met that day
on the Petit Pont,

who insisted they go dancing,
then escorted her to the hotel

and seized her in his coils,
who thrust his hemipenis

into every orifice,
murmuring how snake sex

can take a whole night.
Every scratch from his mating spur

made her want to rip her skin off.
Even when someone came in

he kept going,
laughing at her.

Years, his eggs have stayed inside her,
ready to hatch in this sketchpad:

cobras, cascabels, condas,
tree boas, harlequins.

She strokes the retic –
her hog-swallower.

She fills in the last cross-hatch
on his snout, can feel the skin

loosening around his mouth,
ready for the moult.

She waits for lights-out,
smudges carefully with the eraser,

easing his skin like a dress
pulled over a girl's head,

the pencil of herself
blunt, her work done,

her own face empty
on the pillow beside her.

El Hombre Caimán

I draw and draw
in the therapy class
and snap at those
who try to stop me,

be they iguana, capybara
or you my daughter.
I could tell you how
a man will woo

in an Hombre Caimán
suit. Watch for
that moment when
he raises his snout

and lifts his tail
then bellows.
He'll headslap the water
to get your attention.

That's when the singing starts.
Mesmeric!
Even a mile off you'll feel it
rise through your soles

and up your spine.
The ground-shake's a warning.
You'll be drawn to
the water's edge to see

how he makes drops
dance on his back
with the bone-shivering
waves of his voice,

you'll bathe and he'll watch you,
you'll glimpse the eyeshine
of his red eyes
through the keyhole.

Precious Goliath Beetle

Beetles with intricate
cameras mounted
on their carapaces

record every harm
that comes to her
in diamantine detail.

Buck

The doctor says no but
she knows she's pregnant,
can feel the embryo
hardening like a bullet.

She gives birth while working
in the brewery heaving crates,
brings it home – the fawn –
her blood still wet on his coat.

His father whisks him away
to a wet nurse
in the foundling hospital.
No wonder then

that instead of antlers,
he begins to sprout
rifles, butts first, barrels
pointing at his brain.

Her buck runs into the desert
with his rack of weapons,
even the buds shed velvet
to reveal pistols.

The Birth of Jaguar Girl

You come out hissing,
bite off your own cord,
gobble the afterbirth

and lick me off your fur.

You stumble into the garden
to chew ayahuasca leaves,
get so high

your tail's a fer-de-lance
to play catch with,

your spots tarantulas
pouncing through sunlight.

Your new eyes
are blue as morpho butterflies
drunk on fermented fruit.

When the doctors catch you
you leap up the buttress roots
of their trousers.

They press a black scorpion
against your chest
to listen to your heart –

that spider monkey
swinging through your ribs.

You barely last the day
before they drug you,

my cub-mama, fire-girl,
too dangerous for the ward.

Soon, your mouth fills
with vampire bats
and burrowing owls.

Every time they sedate you
I have to carry you in my belly again,

pad on all fours
over the Pantanal of the corridors.

Months, I grow heavy with your visions,
until it's time to give birth

to my Yaguara Beast,
She-Who-Kills-With-One-Bound –

who claws her way out.

My Amazonian Birth

The arrival of colour – plumes of it piercing your lungs
as you take a first breath,

your eyes like thistles of light
that whirl,
            wondering
where shall we root?

Now, sunrays are the wings
of macaws,
            more sound than colour –
the cry that comes out of you is their tails
            flaring across a creek at sunrise.

*

You are dragged from the grove where colours
fly in faithful couples

as your Amazon mama is wheeled away –
her hair a coral tree against institution green.

The rainforest that engulfed you
is pushed away by orderlies,

            as if you're on a boat
            and the riparian walls glide past,

but it's the jungle sliding downstream,
not the boat
fighting the current as it noses the Puna foothills, towards your source.

Everything you need
is carried off on a gurney
to be packed in ice.

Your mama's face is a mudslide
as the septicaemia bites.

*

And your face, moving over the waters?

Your face that was once a rag of rain, slivers of you rearranged
        nightly in her womb,
the splinters sloshing like quicksilver as her fever spikes.

Your face that once was lodged in the mother-tree
        among branch-tributaries and fountains of palms.

Your face where the macaws nested
and the harpy eaglet hatched,

where the sloth crawled across your lips like a tongue on its first
        outing.

One eye is life the other death –
        two armadillos in their burrows.

One cheek is dawn the other dusk –
O the harmonies they sing! In the twilight
of your face-stem, the hum of the singing flower
no one has discovered!

Your mouth where vowels hover like bees!

*

One hand is day the other night.

The feet unfurling like epiphytes,
one shy one brave,
one with a treefrog between its toes, one with a cockroach,
but oh how the roach's armour shines with rubies and garnets!

And the toes that strangers will stroke as if to remember swinging
        through the canopy.
The soles that have not yet walked on concrete
but wriggle to follow an ocelot's trail,

curious for the bounty and the horror, wanting to watch the puma
crack a deer's neck in the hospital car-park.

*

Grief squatting in your heart
like a strangler fig high in a branch-fork,
                        that sends roots
down your chest and weaves a cage
around each hope –

your chest that, even as it's learning to breathe, feels vines tighten.

*

Your jungle-mama floating downstream now
until she reaches a firedoor
swung open then slammed, echoing down the corridor.

What a wind ruffles your caul,
for the river-silt still clings to you
and the uranus moths suck your salts.

A soaring in your head
that's a breakage
as someone wipes off the scat,

        your expression is
                now a flock of disturbed parrots
                now an egg that will not hatch.

A scorpion coils in the theatre lamp,
its sting poised.

*

Your bud-ears
hear the crash
as she reaches ICU
        so laden with orchids
        she topples to the floor.

There she lies, her roots upended like jangled nerves
they'll diagnose as anxiety
that slides into psychosis.

Butterflies jink over her trunk
even as her flesh rots
        and blossoms with fungi –

your broken mama
laid out like a long-table
        for the rest of your life to feast on.

Hummingbird Birth

When I see the rufous
in her nest, about to lay an egg
almost as big as her head,
I think about my birth.

She holds her wings up,
this Thumbelina,
and everything quivers,
she arches her back,

lifts herself over the tiny cup.
She pants, she crosses her wings,
raises them,
lifts her rump.

For half an hour she tries,
which must be forty-eight
in hummer-time.
She opens her beak and I can see

the crimson throat inside.
How much longer can she bear it?
It seems she is going to give birth
to a planet.

Her eyes open and close,
she is looking in.
She squeezes her eyelids shut,
stretches her wings again.

She utters three cheeps.
She fluffs her feathers
and now she leans forward
like a little balloon

that someone is blowing up.
She perches on the nest rim
like it's the edge of the world
and I can see the white egg

behind her – no blood.
There are orange sparks on her throat.
Her back feathers are burning–
green, copper.

My mother's hair was fire,
her throat had a lit patch
as she uttered
her sharp words:

When you finally came out, they
placed you in an incubator
and packed ice all around me.
I almost died of septicaemia.

After you told me that,
I looked at my narrow hips,
bird thighs, and was
too scared to have children.

The hummingbird mother
sits on her eggs –
there are two now.
Perhaps she is exhausted.

If she's torn,
it doesn't stop her
incubating her treasures,
then zipping off to sip nectar

for their first feed.
Like you, she will bring up her chicks alone.
She'll chase off chipmunks,
even humans, stabbing

at their foreheads until she draws blood
if anyone comes close.
After two days' labour
they cut me out of you

and I was sent away,
too young to migrate
for the Mexican winter
from the summer nest in Alaska.

It's not true that I hitched a ride
on the backs of geese
through hurricane and hail.
And although I made it back

to the breeding grounds,
the male, with his
emerald-rust armour, his
rose-copper gorget –

couldn't persuade me
to have children,
even when he turned himself
into a hummingbird

and promised that laying eggs
would be natural as flying.

L'Assistance Publique

What has he done with your babies?
He says they're with welfare services.

What can you do now but sit
on the broken bed
and rock yourself to sleep?

You don't like to think
what he's up to all night,
who he's with, how old they are.

Better to rock the cradle
where a rat is cuddling a doll.
Who called the helpers?

You call them fairies,
they have orchid-twig bodies,
dragonfly wings –

they wind sticky webs
around kicking limbs,
command hornets to sting.

There is torture by insect-people
for the changelings,
my Madonna of Sorrows –

this rat-boy who swings from your breast,
his incisors in your nipple,

this doll-girl who will not say *Mama!*
however much you shake her.

Harpy Eagle Mama

All night I've had my head stuffed
down an armadillo hole, face first,
my bare hide stuck out to be stung
by the thugs of the jungle floor.
By dawn I'm begging for the rain's
knives to finish me off. I long for
a harpy eagle's claws to crush me,
lift me past treetops, crack my skull
by the time she makes the big tree.
There are spines in my cheeks. I'm half
brat half armadillo. When my saviour
lands with that rush through her
giant wings, she grabs my neck
but doesn't snap it, drops me softly
in her nest wide as a double bed,
the mattress spread with monkey fur.
All I do is screech for the pain to stop,
but she hunts for snacks to tempt me,
dangles them over my lips
that gape as if turned to horn.
I take the morning catch, sliver by sliver,
worms of sloth trail from my chin.
I do this day after day now, live on
a diet of maggots and guts – I don't care
that I'm stuck in a cloud, nor
question why the harpy adopted me.
I'm growing strong – pin-feathers
sprout from the sores in my skin.

Baby Caimans

From the Río Negro
you can see her
on the sandbank
playing with her baby caimans as if they're dolls.

She dresses and undresses them, sticks dummies in their mouths,
hums a tune,
this old child who's
been swallowed alive,
her pieces
cut out of daddy

caiman's belly
and put back together too many times,
her flesh stitched
to make a patchwork armour.

She stays there even when the river rises over her head,
when floating trees crack her spine.

The caimans get bigger
and she gets smaller, shrinking to a dot
like a sandfly
on the opposite bank.

From the boat you'll
need binoculars, but
you can't help her.

You'll return in the evening
with flashlights
but all you'll see
are the red eyes of

mummy and daddy
caiman,
only their eyes out of the water,

and on your neck you'll hear a voice, persistent as a sandfly,
hungry for blood.

But if you moor in the mud, the child will torment you
like this bug infected
with leishmaniasis.

Ulcers will erupt in your bites and gnaw your flesh,
eating away your face.

Musica Mundana

Later, when I became a painter of tropical
flowers, the canvases grew vast.
I named one: 'The Language of Flowers
and Mute Things'. Angel's trumpets
dripped down the cloth and mingled with oil.
If a moth flew in it got trapped.
Spiders arrived, dragging their legs
through impasto. I threw in some
baby smocks, and they bloomed,
glowing in the clay-and-straw ground.
I trailed a lock of my mother's hair
and the strands drifted across
as if there was a wind in my Eden,
another maker's breath stirring the plants
that kept changing shape. But it was
only when I added my mother's
ashes that the painting seemed to come
alive. I paced back and forth,
rocked myself into the frame of mind
to hear what paint has to say.
I thought I heard one bud clear its throat
but my ears were too coarse. It was like
being pulled from the earth by the root,
this sound, a snatch of sun-roar.
From the side, the daturas looked like
newborn skulls with their fontanels
poised. Waterlily scalps loomed
from the mud of the marsh.
One night they opened.
Inside each stigmatic cup was an interior
like a doll's house, complete with a lace bed
adorned by the corpses of flies,
their heads propped on pillows.

Limed Blossoms

The lure is flowers, irresistible,
as is his description of each room
in the villa he has rented –
she must give him one more chance.

I have the letter he sent her,
still fragrant from the blooms
he pressed inside. *Come,*
my little hummingbird, he writes,

come to my garden of delight
and lie in its black beds.
A woman can divide herself
into a charm of colibris.

I've seen my mother grow needle-bills
to feed from his floral traps,
flicking her tongues
to drink deep in trumpets.

But a child can't understand
who would paint the insides of corollas
with gummy linseed. I've watched my father
lift the petticoats of lilies

and rub birdlime on their thighs.
A blur of darts, then the struggles
of faces drowning in pollen,
her tails dangling from limed blossoms.

I've dashed from petal to petal
with cotton buds, dissolvent, to free
her warriors, these *chuparosas*
that I now prise, mummies wrapped in tepals.

I remember the sounds those flowers made –
buzzes, squeaks, high-pitched cries
from deep inside each goblet, as if,
at last, my childhood had found a voice.

My Mother's Dressing Gown

At night she wore a rustling affair
with smoky lining, filmy treeferns
overlaid with prickly palms –
it was like having a cloud-forest in the room.

Her face was an axed mahogany.
Her hands emerged from emerald sleeves
to meet on the table, talons tensed,
like a puma challenging a tayra.

Her feet – for Maman wore stilettos indoors –
were the stilt roots of fin-trees
and under her gown she wore a moss basque
with bats clinging to her cleavage.

Lianas encased her figure
in the series of corsets
my father bought her
and her legs were snared in mist-net stockings

lit by diamonds of moonlight
filtering through the sub-canopy.
Her pelvis was a bank riddled with burrows
that Papa dug with his nails.

He loved to surprise her by inventing
new raids on her nests.
She was a smoulder of leaves
in the lee of a bushfire, flat

under the steamrolling man who owned her.
From my cot, I heard cries
only a cornered peccary would make.
I'd wake screaming from night terrors,

then Maman would come, her robe alight,
but Papa would order her back to bed.
And then there'd be nothing
between me and my father.

Square de la Place Dupleix

Your family weaves you on devotion's loom, rick-racking the bed
LES MURRAY

Inside the sandpit you are playing for your life. Your
bucket and spade that smiled all day long, like family
in your satchel, now work hard. Your material is sand. It weaves
a universe where you are huge, the cellar behind you,
eclipsed by twelve chestnut trees and their pigeon gods. On
and on you burrow, into your sanctuary, devotion's
priest. There are rituals to do, like counting leaves on the sky's loom.
Any lapse and you tumble back into the brain's forks, rick-racking
the minutes for the lock that unclicks, the coffining dark, the
hooded stranger with Papa's voice, the makeshift bed.

Her Harpy Eagle Claws

Comfort your mother
Dr Pryce says.

My mama is perched
on top of the wardrobe

growling. She's holding
her spider monkey teddy
in her six-inch talons

the way she used to hold my hand
when we crossed the boulevard

and I let go

because being hit by cars
felt so much safer.

Madre de Dios

I peer down through the plane porthole
    at the river-coils.
        How quickly the clouds
part, and the glass morphs
    into a microscope
        through my zoom lens,
I see a cocoi heron
    pluck a caiman hatchling
        on a bend of the Madre de Dios,
and dash it against rocks
    to gulp it down like spaghetti.

The meanders crumble into oxbows,
    and oh the quiet there where
        the slaughtered snakes sleep. I could
almost forget that high in an ironwood
    a scarlet macaw chick
        squawks for food from its parents
but is ignored. How the primaries
    of beauty and horror
        pack every square inch
like the scales of a rainbow boa,
    how I'm flying towards this

at six hundred miles per hour,
    will be dropped into it,
        while she who gave birth to me
after she was raped by a man
    she calls the cockroach
        will place her palm
on isula ants so as not to feel
    what he's doing, focusing
        on the in-out of the fire-needle.
She'll press her spine
    into a Tangarana bole

and let the fire ants surge
     from under the bark,
          burn her like a saint
to erase where his hands groped.
     My mother, who would slice
          off a breast before
he mauled it, whose movements
     are drugged as a sloth's along
          the snakewood where Azteca
ants teem. She who walks barefoot
     over a file of leafcutters, their leaf-

sails held like protest banners.
     Your father, she'll say one day, *was*
          a cockroach, and cockies can survive
a nuclear blast, nothing
     can blitz his memory. And don't think
          you'll escape, my hungry chick
hiding in your hole inside
     the world's biggest forest. For Cockie
          will find you, in the corner,
bite your unfledged wings
          and eat you alive.

Fossa

There is a beast that runs
naked through the streets,
setting fire to bins,
trying on clothes in stores,

dresses she drops on the pavement
as passers-by gawk,

who throws coins at the crowds
and offers credit cards to kids.

Her tail is long as her body
and helps keep her balanced
as she climbs the stone trunks
of strange cities.

When she was ten
she could fight off gangs,
win every cat-fight,

could skip along jagged-glass walls
as they jeered about her mammy.

When rats leapt over her bed
she caught them.

Now, the doctors ask her who she is
and she says:
I am the fierce fossa
of Madagascar,

I eat your cats and dogs,
my red tail is a torch
that sets fire to your cars.

They ask her again,
as she races around
their consulting rooms.

They keep asking
until she gives the right answer.

Cryptoprocta ferox she bawls
in that voice she keeps for emergencies
like all the males are after her
and she's not ready.

Wrong! They shout, *wrong!*

They shave her red-brown fur
these he-doctors
and again she tries to escape,
to scale the towers of Liverpool, Cardiff...

Still she insists she's the ferocious spirit
of the Kirindy Forest,
the last daughter of her species.

They ask: *Who tamed you?*

She sits on the chair
and growls at the ghost
that's always there

following her down the cobbled alleys.

The Roach, she says, *that
playboy, lie-a-bed*

*who fucked the world
while I worked,*

who tore into me
before I reached the mating tree,

before I offered myself
on the bridal branch, the high one
where I could kick off ugly suitors.

Anaconda

She calls her depression Anaconda,
      she is all tail, pure crush-force.

She throws a coil around her own chest
      and squeezes until her heart bursts,

all thirty feet of her, dragging
      her bulk from the swamp

so slowly, trees grow on her.
      Her eyes can mesmerise a fawn –

which is how vulnerable
      my mother gets before a strike,

the eyes, only the eyes, like a tunnel
     she must crawl towards, the green

and khaki muscles of the void.
      The Sach'amama will eat her whole,

headfirst, clamp recurved teeth
      around her face and draw her in.

Days it takes to pass down her own throat
      and digest each bone. Months

my mother lies in despair's belly –
      almost dissolved in the monster's juices.

Black Caiman with Butterflies

Depression is a black caiman
lying on the sand,

mud-slicked from the deep,
impassive in her armour.

Nothing can get through to her,
she'll lie there for hours, unblinking.

How to explain then
the appearance of butterflies?

Sparking flambeaux, snowy-whites,
at the corner of her eyes,

as if the beauty of the world has come
to perch on her, to drink her tears.

Extrapyramidal Side Effects

Mania

Imagine a mother with a mind
hyper as a rainforest,

the ward echoing with
whoops of titi monkeys,

as a Río Negro bursts
the banks of her cheeks,

her skin prismatic
with an oil spill –

who lights a match
and holds it to her chin.

Haloperidol

She's jittery as a butterfly
drying her new wings.
What started as a shiver
is a permanent tremor –

she lies in the hospital sheets
like a morpho in a bird's beak.

Paranoia

Paranoia is a spectacled caiman
with a horsefly between her eyes.

Largactil

She's been doing the anteater shuffle,
her head bowed to the ground,
her nose stuck in an anthill.

ECT

Every day is the day
the shock-box is wheeled in,

electrodes that think
her tongue is a catfish,

make her teeth clench
like a giant river otter
that's just caught lunch.

Hallucination

I'm her dark mirror
of biting glass, a cloud
of crystal mosquitoes
she swats away.

Occupational Therapy

The art therapist says:
your mum spends her time
making a black jaguar
from the corpses of flies.

Radioactive Iodine

They call it bioluminescence
but she knows she's only a worm
with a luminous green head.

Lithium

Now that her thyroid's burnt away
she floats in her turquoise negligee
like a manatee in a tank.

Depression

What she wants is dawn
but the windows are blacked out
and the oil slick steals across
her eyes like a blindfold.

Terribilis

Here comes Nurse with the trolley.
Here comes the papier-mâché cup

and the meds lined up
like poison dart frogs –

Phyllobates terribilis, the one
that will paralyse

when its candy coat
is placed on her tongue.

Jaguar Mama

1

Once, she was the giant jaguar of my prehistory,
carried me tenderly between sabre teeth,

licked my rosettes until they grew lush
as treeferns draped with black orchids –

the whirlpools and rocks of her tongue
almost pulled my skin off, I never knew

if she was grooming or preparing to eat me.
Her eyes were oxbows in which piranha shoals thrashed.

My painted warrior, who retreated into the wetland
as her power waned, the symmetry of her face

fissioned into a Bosch triptych, wrinkles over her cheeks
like demons no powder could conceal,

demons cascading from the mouths of demons,
wrinkles wielding pitchforks.

2

Sometimes I'd glimpse her drinking her reflection
or reclining on a sandbank as if it was a chaise longue,

a Gitane dangling from her lips like a rolled up rainforest
she'd set on fire during one of her rages.

Give me her rages, her running rampage down the street
naked, rather than this drugged beast

the goldminers taunt, that tourists pay to gawp at.
Give me her razoring stare, the tinfoil glint

in the killing pools of her eyes, not this stingray infested
swamp bordered by bats, mosquito-cloud

cataracts over her eyes. Give me
the mother who runs through the estate

showering money at kids, who unpins tenners
from the flames of her hair.

3

Hold that high, a pale-winged trumpeter's tremolo
vibrating through her even while she sleeps.

Who knows what they dream, these patients
on sleep treatment. They descend to an understorey

bristling with ants, get stung but keep sleeping.
They don't eat for a month, haunted by hoots

of the night monkey. Then the howlers start
their dawn delirium. First one, like the door

of hell wrenched open, then others
and it's a gale ripping through a ship, until

the whole selva is convulsed. The inmates
try to reply but their throats are stuck.

Light, when it filters through her eyelids
is the oropendola's waterdrop-note, a nurse

4

shaking her arm to say *your daughter's come to visit.*
I entered the hospital like a fawn who must be sacrificed.

Better to be torn limb by limb alive
than to be rowed over the stagnant lakes of Mother's eyes.

Give me a telescope's safe distance
to view the jacamar perched on her saline drip,

the screaming piha on her head-board.
Was it lithium or mercury that poisoned her?

that dissolved the oil paintings of onça-pintada,
the face she made up so carefully each morning.

Now her mascara's streaked, her paw shakes.
My mother in her spotted pyjamas,

vicious as a jaguar caught in a trap,
the tranquilliser dart wearing off.

My fierce mama, her teeth in a mug,
hydroelectric dams draped around her neck.

Bottled Macaw

Hyacinth they call me, blue gold,
a chick stuffed in a plastic bottle.

I fret out feathers to give my beak a job,
am naked by arrival,

drunk on the rum they forced down
to keep me dumb during the dark.

My eye peeps out the bottleneck,
too scared to close. But at last

I blink. And when I open
I see the clay-lick rosy as mango,

my breath mists the bottle-sides,
but through the neck it's dawn,

rays lick the leaves awake.
I'm home with my parents, they coddle me

with sun-talk, their tails sparkle
with sapphires. I blink again

and I'm biting sacred medicine.
It will mend me, and all my lost friends

in their bottles, wings broken.
We nuzzle beaks. The chatter!

I call the whole cargo to feed
and they come – parrots in jam-jars,

the baby boas coiled in CD cases,
turtles with heads taped in their shells,

the little hummers sewn into smugglers' shirts.
All of us locked in, doing our silent flying,

keeping the colpa ahead –
the clay caves we carve with our hunger.

Waterlily-Jaguar

Dr Pryce says I set fire to myself last night but I say
the flames are jaguar tails and my cigarette burns are spots.

I have time to hear my brain crackle, then
poof! I'm smoke.

But I keep coming back. I can walk on water, my paws
leave pugmarks on the river like a risen Christ-cat.

I'm euphoric as Xbalanque or the many faces of God A.

In the therapy room I draw twenty self-portraits before lunch,
pin a waterlily on my head and roar!

*

After the Luminal, my body slumps.

Then the voices start – bullfrogs, a guan's grunt
like my neighbour Myfanwy being strangled.

I comfort her in speech scrolls like a Mayan deity.

This is my second month in the Sleep Room.
Ten times they shocked me while I was under but I'm still mad.

According to Matron I'm the goddess of bloodletting.
I've hidden my knife for self-decapitation.

*

Have you seen my plant-face?
My skin is a slow-moving river of watered silk,

my freckles are rosettes, I watch them grow
in the bathroom mirror when Nurse wakes me to wash.

I hear the rhizomes stirring in the bath,
anchoring me while I sway.

My cinquefoils are huge as lily pads,
they flex their under-spines

to grip my flesh – green rafts wide as soup-platters,
their quilted patterns smoothing out.

My neck is thrust forward like a stalk
as the buds of my cheeks open

and mask upon mask peels back
to my under-face where beetles feed.

*

It takes an act of will to make
the flower of my face close again,

no one must see how I clamp the petals shut on insects,
even though I can feel them clambering into me –

cockroaches scuttling through my veins.

By the time Nurse brings me back to bed
there's no trace, except for the slime along the floor,

like the ones slugs leave overnight,
and a smear of pond-ooze from my mouth.

Scarlet Macaws

The scarlet macaws want their red back,
not puce but rich rubescence.
They squawk and growl
for the people to give it back.

They want their green and yellow, the ultramarine
and azure of flight feathers.
They want their green homes to vibrate
against their red plumage.

They don't want to be eaten.
They don't want to be sacrificed.
They don't want to be shot for their celestial light
        and lose their eyes.
They don't want to be called Seven Macaw
        and mark the coming of the dry season
        or the hurricane season.

They don't want to be shot from the world tree
        by the Hero Twins
or be worn by them in a victory headdress.
They don't want to be bred as pets or for trade.

They want to spread their feathers
like the world's riches, a currency
that doesn't cost a thing, that doesn't
        symbolise blood.
They don't want their heads chopped off
        and stuck on poles in city temples.

They say their scarlet hue is life.
They say that every tree is an axis mundi
and all their eyes are suns.
They don't want their heads stuck on human bodies
        for funeral rites.

They don't want their ashes to treat diseases
because no medicine is left, no doctor.

They want to take their place
with the quetzal and the jaguar.
Their feathers are axes,
their feathers are lightning,
their feathers are rain

for everyone, not just the rulers with their royal aviaries.
Sun-macaws are free,
they are prayer-arrows,
Morning Stars,
they are the west wind that brings change.
They are the cardinal directions of health.

Do not bury them in human graves.
Do not bury them as plucked grave-goods
until the country is just a naked carcass
with its wings bound tight around its heart.

Río Tambopata

We are words on a journey
not the inscriptions of settled people

She's so huge this catfish
with her black and white eye startled

like a girl's. What words could say
how a caiman's snout is wedged

in her chest? What language can do this?
But I only alight on the scene

for a moment, before the current pulls me
along, and in any case, someone

is driving the boat, someone navigating,
while I struggle with river-vowels

from which a whiskered giant
might leap, dragged down by a spectacled

dinosaur. All I can do is focus
on the word 'horsefly' – a flying

mare of a beast with wraparound
eyes that bulge zigzag green, as its jaws

scissor into the reptile that has plied
these waters since the dawn of sound.

Uirapuru and the Tangarana Tree

A musician-wren nests in the ant tree,
she sings the world's loneliest song
in her tower patrolled by fire ants.
She charms them when she builds
her vase of leaves, flitting in
the understorey like a woodland spirit.
When she sings, all the birds listen.
None of them can nest here,
even other plants dare not approach
or their leaves are cut by her guards.

Once, a girl was tied naked to the trunk.
The ants that race in tunnels under the bark
swarmed, they injected their venom,
back and forth they rocked, like the needles
of sewing machines, up and down,
then carried fragments off
until there was no more flesh on her.
The uirapuru tells the girl's story
every evening, from her perch
in the solitary tree by the river Iriri.

To hear it, you must stand still as a tree,
must let the red ants crawl night and day
through your marrow, to milk the sap of aphids.
Nectar and formic acid, these are the tones
the wren sings, perfectly twined.
The flutes of each vowel cut through flesh,
until your blood crawls with rivulets of ants.
By dawn, the trunk of your spine is clean,
a clearing around you no one can breach.
Sunlight filters down to flood your bones,
your feet turned to roots, your skin to bark.

Corpse Flower

Some people have mothers,
I have a corpse flower,
her corm buried in the soil of my heart
where every hurt is stored
huge and heavy.
I always know when she's about to erupt
because the sweat bees
land on my face,
flesh-flies crawl in my mouth.
Overnight, she shoots
through the top of my scalp,
rearing into the sky.
I wake to the stench of carrion.
Her one petal surrounding
the monstrous spike
is wide as a ballroom gown,
the pleats meat-red,
the outside green as she once was
when the screw-worm
took her dancing –
frilly wrap-around
that fell away when my father
pushed her face-down on the bed
revealing stigma broderie.
Some people have mothers,
I have a titan arum,
the full skirt of her spathe
rotting until all that's left
is the red stump
bearing toxic fruit.

My Mother's Love

I asked my mother
where she kept her love
and she answered:

My love is a golden bird
in a crystal cage

and that cage is perched
on the head of a fat boa
coiled at the top of a tree

and that tree is surrounded
by scorpions
and tigers and bears.

So I went in search of the tree
and fought the beasts
around its trunk.

I fought the fat snake.
But when I opened the cage

I found a goldcrest
with its wings torn off.

When My Mother Became a Boa

She reared above her bed
and kept on rising
like a boa from a basket.
Her nightdress billowed
with sequinned scales.
Muscles rippled around
the coils of her body
and told her what to do.
She flung the windows open,
the hospital gardens sparkled.
I saw the birds lift out of trees,
like a magnet they flocked to her,
drawn out of the sky
until it was empty.
They fluttered around her face,
she opened her mouth wide,
revealed her curved teeth,
vermilion gums, the roof
of her mouth arched and glistened.
She unhinged her jaws,
swallowed the birds whole,
all the glory of the tropics –
until she'd eaten the world's colours.
But still they kept coming,
they chattered as they flew.
Some perched on the bedrail
before they entered.
When she'd gulped them all
and I could still hear them chattering
inside her, she drew in her tongue,
it flicked on her lips
as she curled back down
under her bedclothes, swollen,
sleepy, and closed her slit-pupils.

Other patients' visitors murmured,
they drank tea from the trolley
as nurses did their rounds
but no one saw what had happened.

Mama Ferox

Today, her teacup is a bromeliad
filled with crystal blue florets,

her drip is a pod
hanging from the camphor tree.

She hasn't slept for weeks,
she's restless as an orchid

growing on a wasps' nest.
Adrift on her Río Loco

she enters a stretch
no other human has braved.

It isn't the howler monkey's roar
that sends her spinning over the cataracts,

nor the spine-tingling growls
the male makes,

pelting her with his dung,
as if the last stronghold of virgin land

has found a voice –
red-furred, ferox –

clearing the soil from its throat
to defend its den.

No, this is not the signal.
The slow descending scales

of the grey potoo
in the lull afterwards begins it,

steam rising from the treetops
like a nightdress whipped off,

the rough clothes of day
marching in,

even the hairs on Nurse's hands
that turn into spines – these are the signals,

as the rest of the ward goes quiet,
the curtains drawn around her bed

like waterfalls she must crawl behind
along a slippery ledge.

The falls, she knows, have frozen.
It is she who is pouring, who is being poured

so fast that her skin smokes
in pellets of scattergun spray.

The Hospital Haircut

When I last saw my mother she was sitting
inside a shaft of sunlight,
her auburn hair still red.
The hospital hairdresser drew up
strands so fine it was like
looking at fibre-optic threads.
Maman's eyes were closed,
the corners of her lips trembled.
The freckles on her face were lit
like the spots on a deer
but her skin was pale as a python
that has spent its entire life
under a heat-lamp in a tank.
She opened her eyes and saw me –
I had not visited for years.
Her hazel irises were cages
for creatures that wanted to break out
and eat me. When she spoke,
her mouth was the place where a python
tries to swallow a doe
then vomits it because it's too large.
The hairdresser continued combing
through all this, the curls sparked
as if they wanted to sprout antlers –
those chignons of her glamorous past
she'd tamed with backcombing
and Elnett and a thousand pins.
Maman acknowledged me
then she closed herself to all
but the kind hands that stroked.
Her tongue flicked over her dry lips
like a snake's, but I knew
it was the tongue that had talked
to angels as they swept their great wings
over her forehead when she was nine.

My child-mother with the sheet
pulled over her face, against
the wingtip piercing her small window,
the miracle of how such a vast being
could get through. Then the icy touch
on her brow, that let in the visions –
the fairies that danced on her ceiling.
When she lifted her glance to me one last time,
all I heard was the snip of the scissors,
all I saw were filaments fluttering
in a halo around her head –
her fairy wings, angel feathers,
fallen on the floor.
And her thoughts locked inside
her now cropped scalp, like a wildfire.

Zarafa the First Giraffe in France

When Maman stood in front of the crowd
and blurted her life story

it was as if the first giraffe
had arrived in Paris.

They stared at her long neck.
Zarafa, gift from the Egyptian Pasha –

she's walked all the way from Marseille,
six hundred miles

with a cage of antelopes
and mouflons, two cows,

a mounted police escort.
My mother, who announced she was so

tired from sleeping upright
only five minutes at a time,

from trotting past gawking hordes
who saw a camelopard

with a kick that could kill a lion
if approached too suddenly.

My 'beautiful animal of the king'
led by three ropes

and a retinue of carers,
her limbs elongated

like a crucifixion
by El Greco.

I was too embarrassed to own her —
my mama

who spent the rest of her life
in a menagerie.

Great Grey Owl

Ménagerie, Jardin des Plantes

If I can hold the stare of this owl
as if looking at my mother,
that silent phantom of my north
who sometimes visits me
in the taiga of my bed,
who snaps her beak, spreads
her wings and growls, this spectre
who can spot prey a mile off, if
I can be brave enough
I will follow her to her nest
lined with wolf hair. I will climb
into that home, between bones
of weasels and crows. Pine
is the scent that brings it back.
Let me be so close that I can see
the concentric rings of her facial discs,
the two mazes that lead me
to the white X at the centre,
the dilated black pupils in gold foil,
the horn bill below. I raise
my eyes to hers – to a will
that can drive away a bear. Then
I take off with her, gliding low
over the wolverine wilderness. She is
teaching me to hear the heartbeat
of voles beneath drifts. We dive,
crashing through pack snow
to grab what we can.
If I can hold her stare
and nestle against her breast –
but my ash ghost is gone.
One feather floats down through the bars,
while the chouette lapone
who's turned her head right around
has dismissed me.

Ocelot

She's a tangle of bars and dots
someone has smeared on her coat
while she was running. Or,
as Dalí would have said –
so as not to frighten his guests –
she's just a housecat I've painted over
with an op art design. Babou,
it's rumoured, only smiled once,
when she was escaping. If I think
of your leash and jewelled collar,
and of your bids for freedom –
I'd want to meet the artist
who can take his brush
into your infested jungle, just
to catch the ringed tail, the phosphor
on leaves as you pass,
my ocelot mother, tigrillo,
not much yourself in your life,
more an afterthought the psychiatrist
jots in his notes, concluding
this patient is beyond diagnosis.

Kapok

It's only when the queen of the forest
has fallen that we see how many crutches
she needed to keep upright –
her mesh of roots pulled up
the topsoil and it's shallow as felt.
Where was she going in her walking frame?
These buttresses and vines she leant against
didn't help her move forward
and why should she? Here
she had her portion of sun; there
was the darkness of others. No,
she moved upwards, turning her stiff
body into a ladder to climb towards
the leaves of light in their spiral groves,
her face so furrowed no one noticed it.
What burdens she bore to keep her back
upright: the harpies in their heavy nest
pressed on her shoulder,
capuchins inside her armpits.
Tamanduas, toucans, trogons –
all clung to her. And her skin had growths –
a termite's nest, a beehive.
Tree porcupines dozed in her clefts,
a jaguar slept on her lowest limb,
and lower still a bushmaster curled between her toes.
The treefrogs in their bromeliad ponds
multiplied every year, and always,
processions of army ants plagued her.
But it wasn't these lodgers that felled her –
it was the hanging gardens of orchids draped
on her balconies, like worshippers in a cathedral
kneeling in pews, throngs of them
drinking the rain that filtered softly
through her storeys, like sacramental wine,
their faces lifted to divine moths.

Ah Puch

(for Alan Rabinowitz)

For he bites the bars of my trap, breaks his top canines,
his nerves jangling from the stubs.

For I pump him with penicillin and release him
with a wish that he heals as I lose his signal.

For the day comes that he returns
with his radio collar loose,

his ribs poking through matted fur.
For then I run to him and cradle his head

and smell the fetid breath of jaguar.
For with his last strength he clamps

his jaw shut on my finger
but is so weak I can retrieve it,

my blood mingling with his saliva.
For I lift him still alive on my shoulders

and carry him to my hut
even as his claws gouge my back.

For I sit beside him and keep watch.
For we stay a long time by the jars of scat,

the cast of my footprint with his holy paw-print inside it.
For I remember finding that omen on the path –

proof one of his kind was tracking me,
he who is always next to me, his breath in my face

like steam from earth's first dawn
which I breathe as prayer.

For in that stinking fragrance he has teeth
that crack Death's skull,

for I named him after the Mayan god of death, Ah Puch.
For in the house of shadows

he wears a coat of black passionflowers from his private garden.
And he has claws that could tear out my heart

with one swipe, should he wish to.
For he has a curious tail, the tip twitching its question

when he sniffs the human.
For as I carry him to his resting place

he grows heavier with every step.
For he has bathed in the lake

that returns the flesh of eaten animals
to their bones,

he has drunk the vine
that makes blood flow back up veins.

For his roar has entered the sacred trumpets
and when I blow on them

the Amazon regrows
from a heap of dust.

For even his echo
can make a cedar rise from its stump.

For after I kill him with the syringe
I carry him to his favourite tree.

Snow Leopard Woman

I was a trespasser in her secret world
and she was just a smur of smoke on scree,

the owner of wilderness – the mother
with a tail long as her body, thick

as a glacier to wrap round her face.
She had snow-paws for treading on drifts.

Her skin was a velour of icicles
so fine I daren't touch her

as she retreated into her mute zone,
but she chuffed at the mountain

that was always at her side,
her Altai, her Himalaya

where she let her mind soar.
I'd sit next to her in the Day Room –

my grey ghost with that frost-fire
her eyes shot at me so I felt scorched.

Where she hid was always minus thirty
but exposed to pure sun. She knew

traps were set below the snowline
so she climbed higher, up above the icefield

towards the summit,
until there was no more up.

In the Giraffe House

Visiting you in the hospital
is like going into the giraffe house,
to peer down into that deep pit
where they overwinter.
Your head sways towards me,
a map of *terra incognita*.
Your legs wade as if through the sea –
my clown-on-stilts, sleepwalker
in desert pyjamas, your eyes too soft,
your mouth so slack the upper jaw
moves away from the lower
like you've taken out dentures
but have to chew over the same word.
If only you could remember who this visitor is
high up in the viewing gallery.
I want to commemorate your youth
in the savannah, my giraffe mother.
I'm only passing through to shelter
from the cold. It's freezing outside
and I wanted warmth
but you are all the colours of drought,
the cracked riverbeds of your skin
a jigsaw no one can get right.
I rest my palm against the partition
and my breath blurs your lips, the long
blue tongue that keeps licking the glass.

Mama Macaw

An egg with the blue-and-gold chick
of a planet inside

is what Mama Macaw dreams of
as she flies through space

searching for a mate. She knows
what she'll do when she finds him –

pluck down from her breast,
tender tips from her tail,

to line a nest in the night-tree.
She knows her chick will be the last

of her species, the last speaker
of earth's tribe. Her chick's wings

will be sunset and sunrise,
her head will stream with auroras.

Rebirth of the Rainforest

A doe comes to the riverbed
bearing a felled forest on her back.

She bends down to drink
the river of stars that is rising
in a snake of mist.

The fawn inside her stirs,
her pelt flowering with rain.

*O my daughter, stay safe
through the storm*, the deer says,

and the baby forest's horns
begin their velvet mosses,
fern-spores lace her head.

My Wolverine

When my mother says I was her kit
taken from her too early,
I think not of cats but a wolverine,
my devourer of snowfields, who,
when she can find no more prey,
eats herself, even the frozen bones.
I crawl down the black phone line
as if it's an umbilicus
to the last refuge on our planet,
towards whatever back country
happens to be her territory today.
My nails remember to claw.
I lope up the icefall
she's retreated to, that's melting behind her
as she climbs her precipice, too drunk
on freedom to come down.
She shows me the den where words are born
fighting. I do not blame her.
I hold the receiver against my face
as if it's her muzzle, her reek
of blizzard-breath. I embrace
the backward-barbed teeth that can
fell a moose and gnaw even its hooves.
Kit – she spits the word out
in a half-love half-snarl and I
am her glutton, scavenging on my yelp
when I was torn from her after birth,
and again now – not long before she dies.

The Hummingbird Whisperer

Let the surgeon who opens my mother
be tender as a hummingbird whisperer.
Let him pull back the walls of her abdomen
and see uncut jewels under his knife.
Let him have a pet name for each part –
his hummers, oiseaux mouches,
his beija-flores, colibris, his almost
extinct hooded visorbearer.
Let him handle them with crystal instruments,
easing droppers down each throat
to check their stomach contents are rich
in micro insects and spider eggs,
the nectar of never-before-seen orchids.
Let him soothe them as their black eyes
turn to watch him. Let them be so calm he can
unwrap their dressings to measure their wings
and wipe blood from their feathers.
Let him clean each gorget and crest
so the colours shine with health.
Let my mother's dryads and sylphs,
hermits and Incas, her sapphires,
her ruby-topaz moustiques,
practise flying again – forwards, backwards,
on the spot, hovering and hyperactive
to the last in their silk compartments.
Let their dissolvable straitjackets
drop off at the appointed time. Let
the man who closes my mother's body
check that each flight feather is intact
and return her to the recovery room to land safely.

Mama Oceana

I ask: what is my mother now?
and the forest answers
with a letter written
in dew on a leaf

where I'm reflected
in a drop of sunlight
like a trembling embryo
held safe by Earth's wet skin.

Musician-Wren

My mother, who today is just
a coat hung on the line –

let me be a musician-wren
and nest in your pocket

to sing you these fluted notes
straight from the forest's throat.

King Vultures

It starts as a fragment of sky
that detaches itself from the stratosphere,
something in my eye as I look up.
I call it the Land of the Dead,
its messenger gliding towards me,
star-ermine cape scalloped with black wings,
to land at the foot of the kapok tree
between buttresses
that remind me of the house we lived in once –
you said a gale had ripped off its roof.

Furniture inside for the afterlife –
and you laid out on the table,
a skeleton curled like a foetus
that the king vultures pierce,
their beaks inside your bowel,
their heads painted with prisms,
their white eyes haloed with red.
Kings of light
who once wore the constellations as headdresses,
death eaters
now bringing up lumps of your flesh,
putrid at first, then sweet.
Flies buzz back to their pupas, maggots shrink into eggs.

If I sniff I can smell the stink that's followed me ever since you died.
Who knows what the mind can do
but here your corpse
is becoming fragrant,
your face pointed east where the sun rises
as our family arrives,
their tears flowing up, back into their eyes,
their tissues folded into pockets.
They hug each other then carry you
into the hut, remove the herbs

packed in your heart, your intestines.
A brush paints backwards, removing the annatto dye
that's protected me against your ghost,
dressing me in red jaguar clothes.

Now the surgeons arrive, scrub their hands, peel on stained
white gloves and green masks
and unpick the stitches across your abdomen,
a scalpel erases its cut,
iodine is wiped off your skin.
You wake as you are counting backwards. When you get to one,
the anaesthetist's needle pops out of the cannula on your hand
and as the gurney is wheeled down corridors
the sedative wears off.
Now you're back in the ward, anti-psychotics
sucked out of your blood into the saline drip.
Poisons rush up syringes; pills appear on your tongue
and fly back into nurses' hands.
Your teeth plant themselves in your gums
and you menstruate.
Wrinkles smooth themselves out
as your hair grows auburn.

Here comes the hard part, the Land of the Dead
floating just above my head
because all along as you've been healing
I've been getting smaller until
I'm a newborn, resting against
the buttress of your thigh, a liana
linking me to you from my navel.
The kapok tree drops a shower of red blooms around me
as I cry out and take a sharp breath.
I'm lifted up, lowered into the ledge of your womb
where I settle in a foetal position facing east.
The king vultures have followed me in
and someone is zipping up my roof with a scalpel.
I squeeze my eyelids shut and my eyes sink into their sockets
then vanish.

My lips close and fuse.
My ears no longer hear your heart.
Silence.

I've gone back as far as I can. You must do the work now
my pregnant mother, you who once told me
what your psychiatrist said – that
you should never have had children.
You were crying at the time and I consoled you
in the hall of my bedsit, cradling the black phone.
The vultures stayed with me all my life. I wake some nights
and their starry heads are above me, as they were
when I lay inside you, my organs shining in the dark
like caskets of jewels to be plundered.

The Hummingbird Nest

I bring you a hummingbird's nest, woven
from seed-down, thistle head,

bound with lichen and spidersilk,
shaped by a mother who presses her breast

against the cup, uses her rump, chin,
the curve of her wing, who stomps

her claws on the base to check it's
windproof under this leaf porch.

The male gone, she works alone,
hurrying back and forth thirty times

an hour, before the eggs come.
She lays them in a home small as a nutshell,

the rim turned in, the sides pliant
so they'll stretch as the chicks grow.

Little mother, I've read your file
filled with letters to the mairie, begging

for a place where we could live together.
I know now how hard you fought the powers,

like a jewelled dart stabbing at their door,
before you fell prey to the jungle mantis.

Instead of flowers, I leave you this nest
on your grave, in case you make it

from your migration – only a wisp
of feathers, no flesh left on your bones.

The Jaguar

Como un río de tigres enterrados

PABLO NERUDA, *Alturas de Macchu Picchu*

He lay on driftwood, the river below him
as if he had cast it off –

the apricot river rosetted
with the pads of waterlilies,
its nap lifted by a dawn breeze.

> His whiskers were old as horsetails,
> his lashes ferns bordering
> the swamps of his eyes.

I crouched in my boat –
no one had been here before,
I would not come again.

The forest swayed with tattoos
of light and shade, no and yes.

And everywhere there were eyes,
rainclouds of eyes, terror-struck,

as if the first human opened hers
and saw mist rising
from her mother's flanks.

My baby self saw the archangel-beast,
the one who arrived to help
with my birth,

> whose irises are hoar forests,
> whose teeth are the pain-price,
> whose roar is the earth
> opening its gates,

the boat of my skin rocking
its hallelujahs,
as it navigated the passage
through and away from Mama.

Like a river of buried jaguars,
the day said,
      a river you have to dive into
      and swim the length of,
      squeezing between the corpses.

ACKNOWLEDGEMENTS

My thanks to the editors of the following publications, where some of these poems were first published, sometimes in other versions: *Agenda, Berfrois, The Compass, The Emma Press Book of Beasts* (The Emma Press, 2017), *The Golden Shovel Anthology* (University of Arkansas Press, 2017), *www.granta.com, Guernica* (USA), *Interlitq, The Manhattan Review* (USA), *New Boots and Pantisocracies* (Smokestack Books, 2016), *New Statesman, The Normal School* (USA), *Oxford Poetry, Ploughshares* (USA), *Poem, Poetry* (USA), *Poetry London, The Poetry Review, Poetry Salzburg Review, Poetry Wales, Quadrant* (Australia), *Queen Mob's Teahouse, Quiet Lunch* (USA), and *The Rialto*.

Some of these poems respond to artworks by visual artists: 'Buck' is inspired by the collage 'Cervus armatus' by Daniel Horowitz; 'When My Mother Became a Boa' is after Walton Ford's painting 'Rhyndacus'; 'Bestiarum' is inspired by his Bête du Gévaudan series at the Musée de la Chasse et de la Nature in Paris; 'Bandaged Bambi' is a response to the sculpture 'Bandaged Bambi' by Julien Salaud; 'Chaplet' is after the photograph 'Chaplet' by Alice Maher; 'My Mother's Wedding Dress' is inspired by Louise Richardson's drawing 'Spun'; and 'Musica Mundana' draws on Anselm Kiefer's 'The Language of Flowers and Mute Things'. 'Birth of the Rainforest' was inspired by Adrián Villar Rojas's installation 'The Most Beautiful of All Mothers'.

The editors of Stonewood Press commissioned 'Mama Oceana' for their 'Traverse: Poetry Trading Cards' series. The epigraph to 'Río Tambopata' is from W.S. Merwin's poem 'An Encampment at Morning' (*Migration: New & Selected Poems*, Copper Canyon Press, 2005). The epigraph to 'Square de la Place Dupleix' is from Les Murray's poem 'Cotton Flannelette' (*Subhuman Redneck*

Poems, Carcanet Press, 1996) and is in the golden shovel form, using Murray's line, for *The Golden Shovel Anthology* (University of Arkansas Press, 2017).

I am grateful to Arts Council England for a generous grant for the arts to allow me time to finish this book, and to travel to Tambopata Research Centre in the Peruvian Amazon for research in the pristine primary forest of Tambopata National Reserve, in Madre de Dios region. Thanks to Berli Carpio, my guide on my first trip there, and to Paul Francisco Condori Vilca (aka Jungle Paul), my guide on my second trip. I'm grateful for their deep knowledge of the fauna and flora. Thanks to Laura Macedo for being so welcoming at the lodge, and to the organisers Rainforest Expeditions. The jaguar poems wouldn't exist without Aramis and Simara at Parc Zoologique de Paris, and the male I was fortunate to see in the wild. Most of the animals featured in these poems I either observed in the wild or are residents of the Parc Zoologique or Ménagerie of the Jardin des Plantes.

I am grateful to the wonderful Gladstone's Library for a month's residency in April 2015, which allowed me concentrated time to write.

Finally, thanks to my editor Neil Astley of Bloodaxe Books for his crucial encouragement and editing, and to Brian Fraser for his patient comments on the poems.

Printed in the USA
CPSIA information can be obtained
at www.ICGtesting.com
JSHW082221140824
68134JS00015B/666